# VEGETARIAN COOKING
# Made Easy
### By Saaudiah Muhammad

# PREFACE

This book is dedicated to my dear mother, and MFM, THEM and HMLF. I am so thankful for having a mother who was the BEST cook ever, in my humble opinion! Everything she made was from scratch. I have fond memories of being in the kitchen and soaking in all of her knowledge and wisdom. I would literally sit and watch her do her magic with the food. She *never* measured anything, she just knew it was right and it would be delicious.

My love for food began at an early age eating cakes, pies, lasagnas, soups and all kinds of yummy foods. With every bite, I grew more in love with my mother and her wonderful cooking. Though I sat and soaked in all of her knowledge while making her decadent delights I never had a desire to cook at All!

My desire to cook and be a good cook came by entering a class of sisters called the M.G.T. & G.C.C. I am so thankful for having a class that teaches me how to be a better sister, mother, and wife. Were it not for MFM, THEM and HMLF, I would not have had the desire to cook, just the desire to eat (smile). I am so thankful for How to Eat to Live (Books 1 and 2) that gave me the inspiration to cook healthy meals. These books have absolutely changed my life and my perspective. I am a blessed woman because I am eating to Live and not eating to Die.

The recipes have been revised and improved upon from the last time that this book was originally published.

It is my hope that you will enjoy the recipes in this book. The goal of this book is to help inspire you to create meals that you and your family will enjoy. You will, hopefully, have entrees or side dishes that you can serve to all because it's just good food, not just vegetarian food. Thank You for your purchase.

Saaudiah Muhammad  :-)

# TABLE OF CONTENTS

Saaudiah Muhammad

# THE WONDERFUL WORLD
# OF LENTILS

**Lentils have a low glycemic index, once consumed they release energy slowly over a long period of time, you will also feel fuller for longer which makes them great for helping you lose weight.** Lentils contain more folate than any other unfortified plant food. In addition to protecting against coronary artery disease by lowering levels of homocysteine in the blood, folate helps prevent birth defects. And folate coupled with vitamin B6 (also plentiful in lentils) may help reduce women's risk of developing breast cancer. Lentils also deliver an impressive amount of blood-fortifying iron -- especially when paired with a food containing vitamin C, such as citrus fruits or peppers. And like other legumes, lentils are a significant (and virtually fat-free) source of protein.

## Heart Health

Studies have found that people who eat high fiber legumes like lentils have a much-reduced risk of heart disease. The high levels of folate and magnesium in lentils also go a long way in protecting the heart.

## Stabilize Blood Sugar

Due to their high fiber content, lentils help in regulating blood sugar by providing steady, slow-burning energy and balancing blood sugar levels.

## High in Iron

Lentils are loaded with iron and are a great way to replenish the body's iron stores, especially for people who don't eat red meat like vegans and vegetarians.

## B Vitamins

Lentils are a great source of B vitamins, most notably folate and niacin (B3). B vitamins are important for the healthy functioning of the nervous, digestive, and immune systems.

## Lower Cholesterol

Lentils are great cholesterol lowering food due to their high levels of fiber.

## Protein Packed

Protein makes up 26% of the calories in lentils and they have the third highest level of protein than any other plant food. It's no wonder that they're a staple in many parts of the world.

Saaudiah Muhammad

*http://www.healthdiaries.com/eatthis/6-health-benefits-of-lentils.html*

# RED LENTIL BURGERS

*Ingredients:*

1 cup of Red Lentils

½ Bell Pepper (any color) diced in small pieces

1 to 2 Garlic cloves minced

½ TSP Cumin

1 TBSP organic Taco Seasoning

1 large Egg

1 ¼ cup all-purpose Flour

½ cup grated Parmesan Cheese

1 Tbsp Olive oil plus oil for sautéing

Dash of cayenne

Salt as needed (Note: *taco seasoning will have sodium so be sure not to use too much additional sodium*)

*Directions:*

Cook red lentils until tender. Drain all liquid and set aside in a bowl. Add bell peppers and garlic in olive oil, then add to lentils. Continue to let the mixture cool. Add all seasonings (salt, cayenne, taco, cumin) to lentils. Beat egg and add to mixture. Add olive oil. Add flour. With a large spoon, carefully place scoops of the mixture in skillet with olive oil on a low-medium temperature.

These patties can be fried, grilled or baked. If frying, fry in olive oil until both sides are golden and slightly crispy. **\*\*\*Regardless of your cooking method...DO NOT Overcook\*\*\*** These go well with broccoli, spinach or homemade fries (either potato or zucchini). You can also place on a bun, add cheese, onions, ketchup, mustard and have a great "burger". This can also be served with your favorite veggie side dishes.

Notes:  As a variation, instead of 1 cup of red lentils, use a ½ cup and add in ½ cup quinoa. Cook them both together and continue with recipe.

## Lentil **"Meatballs"**

*Ingredients:*
**Red Lentil Burger** ingredients
1 TSP each Oregano, Thyme, and Basil
2 Tablespoon of Tomato Paste
¼ all-purpose Flour
Extra Virgin Olive Oil for frying

*Directions:*

Refer to the Lentil Burger Recipe as the base for this recipe. Omit the cumin and taco seasoning.

Add tomato paste to the mixture. Add all the herbs. Combine well. Add the additional flour. Form 1 inch to 1 ½ balls and fry until golden brown on all sides.

Serve with marinara sauce on a submarine bun or serve with pasta for spaghetti and "meatballs."

Saaudiah Muhammad

**Lentil Meatballs**

# VEGETARIAN TACO SALAD

*Ingredients:*

1 cup Brown Lentils

2 cups of Water

Organic Taco Seasoning (1/3 to 1/2 packet)

2 Tablespoon Olive Oil

2-3 TBSP Tomato Paste

1 Avocado (diced)

1 Diced Tomatoes

1 can Black Olives drained and rinsed

Lettuce (any blend of your choice)

Shredded Cheese (Cheddar, Colby etc.)

1 can Corn (optional)

Salt as needed (for the lentils)

Tortilla Chips

*Directions:*

Cook rinsed lentils in water until tender and done about 30 to 40 minutes. Drain cooked lentils. After lentils are fully drained, mash them. You can use the back of a large serving spoon or a clean object with a flat surface to get the lentils out of their hull.

Add taco seasonings. Add tomato paste. Add olive oil to the mixture. Combine lentil mixture well. The mixture should begin to resemble "ground beef".

Once the mixture is ready, begin to build your taco salad, placing lentils atop the lettuce. You can vary the order in which you place the remaining ingredients around the salad. Add lettuce. Add lentils.

Serve chips on the outer edge of your plate.

# Red Lentil "Sloppy Joes"
*This delectable childhood favorite was reintroduced to me via a Vegan recipe group I am a part of...I tweaked this recipe to suit my taste.*

*Ingredients:*

2 cups Red Lentils

1 Red Bell Pepper

1 Small White Onion

1 Clove of Garlic

1 can Organic Tomato Sauce (8 oz)

2 Tablespoon Sun-dried Tomatoes chopped fine

1 Tablespoon Maple Syrup

2 Tablespoon Brown Mustard

1 TSP Basil

1 TSP Thyme

2 TSP Paprika

1 TSP Cumin

Salt and Pepper to taste

Olive Oil to sauté

Whole Wheat or Gluten Free Buns

*Directions:*

Wash lentils and combine with 4 cups of water. Set aside once done. Cook for 20 minutes. In a frying pan add olive oil and sauté bell pepper, onion, and garlic until softened. Stir in tomato sauce, mustard, maple syrup, and spices. Simmer to 10 minutes. Add sloppy joe sauce to the pot with lentils. Stir well then add sun-dried tomatoes. Let cook on low flame for 5 minutes. Toast buns. Place sloppy joes atop buns. Serve with zucchini fries, french fries or chips (potato or veggie).

As a variation, try serving these on slider buns. Sloppy Joe sliders would be a great appetizer for a party or get together with friends and family.

# THE WONDERFUL WORLD
# OF SPINACH!

**Health Benefits of Spinach:**

1. Spinach contains choline and inositol, the substances that help to prevent atherosclerosis or thickening and hardening of arteries.

2. Spinach is loaded with flavonoid that functions as an antioxidant and anti-cancer agent.

3. Spinach contains carotenoid that help fights cancer.

4. Spinach is a rich source of Vitamins C and A

5. Spinach is an anti-aging vegetable.

6. Spinach is a good source of Vitamin K, which aids in the formation of the blood substance required for clotting of blood.

Spinach is also helpful in the following cases; Anemia, Tumors, Constipation, Insomnia, Obesity, Neuritis (inflammation of nerves), Nerve exhaustion, High blood pressure, Bronchitis, Colon cancer, Prostate cancer, Breast cancer, Osteoporosis, Dyspepsia (chronic indigestion), Also helps ailment of the kidneys, bladder, and liver.

*http://len7288.hubpages.com/hub/Health_Benefits_of_Spinach*

# SAUTÉED SPINACH

*Ingredients:*

1 lb. Spinach (fresh or frozen)

1 ½ to 2 TBSP Olive Oil

¼ TSP Nutmeg

1 clove of Garlic finely chopped

½ TSP Salt

½ Lemon

Dash of Pepper

In a large sauté pan, add olive oil and heat on low- medium heat. Add garlic, then add spinach. The pan will appear to be overflowing with spinach (if using fresh), however, the spinach will cook down in about 5-8 minutes or so. Add salt, nutmeg, and pepper. Squeeze lemon over spinach. Serve and enjoy!

# A'ISHAH'S CRUSTLESS SPINACH QUICHE

*This recipe is inspired by my dear Sister A'ishah :-)*

*Ingredients:*

1 pound of fresh Spinach (frozen can be used)

½ TSP Nutmeg

2 Eggs

1 ½ Milk/ Half and Half

1 medium White Onion-Diced

2 cloves Garlic

⅓ cup Olive Oil

1 cup of Flour (all-purpose flour)

2 ½ cups of grated Cheese (Cheddar and Swiss or any kind you prefer)

2 TSP each dried Basil and Oregano

2 TSP Garlic Powder

1 TBSP Tomato Paste

Salt and White Pepper to taste

*Directions:*

Cook 1 pound of spinach with a medium onion finely chopped. Cool, drain as much liquid as possible and place in mixing bowl. Add 2 med to large eggs and mix thoroughly (make sure the spinach is cooled). Add milk/cream Add olive oil…. Add cheese. Add flour.  Add garlic powder, basil, oregano and salt and pepper. Pour in a greased quiche dish…Bake at 350 for about 40 minutes (cooking times may vary slightly). If you want to use a crust simply pour the mixture in a prepared wheat crust. Let rest 15-20 minutes before devouring.

16

Note: You can use just one kind of cheese but I love the tanginess of swiss cheese that can add a delightful "bite" to the quiche.

# CREAMED SPINACH

*Ingredients:*
1 lb Spinach (fresh or frozen)
¼ TSP Nutmeg
4 oz Cream Cheese (softened)
¼ to ½ cup grated Parmesan Cheese
2 TBSP Cream (Half and Half)
1 ½ to 2 TBSP Olive Oil
1 small Shallot
½ TSP Salt
Pepper to taste

*Directions:*
See Sautéed Spinach Recipe and prepare. Add chopped shallot.
Add cream cheese and cheddar cheese. Serve warm. Enjoy!

As a variation, you can add tomatoes to this recipe. Sauté the
tomatoes with the garlic cloves then proceed with the additional
ingredients.

**Creamed Spinach**

# SPINACH ARTICHOKE DIP/BAKE

*This is the recipe from my sister Kati, affectionately known as Kati-Wati. She made this for a bridal shower and it was all the rage! Normally I do not use frozen spinach though it is a viable option, I will make an exception in the case. I definitely knew I wanted to have this recipe in this book!*

*Ingredients:*

1 cup of Mayonnaise

2 pkgs of frozen Spinach

2 pkgs of Cream Cheese

1 pkg of Mozzarella Cheese

1 jar of Artichokes

1 cup of Parmesan

½ cup of Cheddar Cheese for garnish

1 TBSP of Basil

Salt/Pepper to taste

2 clove Garlic minced fresh or 1 tsp of garlic powder or 1 or 2 cloves of minced garlic

1 TSP of sugar (optional)

3 TBSP Sun-dried Tomatoes packed in Olive Oil (optional)

*Directions:*

Combine the mayo, cream cheese 1/2 pkg. of the mozzarella, Parmesan, basil, salt and pepper and sugar in a bowl. Fold in the spinach and chopped artichokes, top with the remaining mozzarella and cheddar cheese. Place in a greased baking dish, bake for about 25 to 30 minutes.

# THE WONDERFUL WORLD
# OF ZUCCHINI

Health Benefits:

- Zucchini contains Vitamin C and lutein which promotes eye health.
- Zucchini has low calories which is good for people who want to lose weight. One zucchini has just 25 calories or approximately 15 calories per 100g.
- Zucchini helps to cure asthma as it contains Vitamin C.
- Zucchini helps to prevent diseases, like scurvy, bruising etc., caused by the deficiency of Vitamin C.
- Zucchini, when taken regularly, can effectively lower high homocysteine levels.
- Zucchini also prevents the risk of having multiple sclerosis (MS).
- Zucchini's high water content is perfect for people on diet.
- Zucchini contains good amounts of folate, potassium, and vitamin A important for good health.
- Zucchini can help protect against colon cancer.

*http://len7288.hubpages.com/hub/Health-Benefits-of-Zucchini*

# BAKED ZUCCHINI MEDALLIONS

*Ingredients:*
2-3 Zucchini
1 beaten Egg plus ½ cup of water
1 ½ c of all-purpose Flour
½ c uncooked Farina
1 tsp dried Basil
1 tsp Oregano
Salt/Pepper to taste
Olive oil to drizzle

*Directions:*
Preheat oven to 400 degrees.

Cut washed zucchini in ¼ inch rounds. Combine beaten egg and water in a bowl. Set aside. Combine flour, farina, and spices in a bowl. Dip zucchini slices in egg wash. Then dip in farina mixture.

Place zucchini in a shallow pan or cookie sheet lined with olive oil. Add more olive oil to the zucchini and bake for 30 minutes or until golden brown and crispy.

This can be served as an appetizer with a marinara dipping sauce or as the base for *Zucchini Parmesan* (See next recipe).

# ZUCCHINI PARMESAN

*Ingredients:*

Cooked *Zucchini Medallions*

**Semi-Homemade Pasta Sauce (see recipe)** or 1 jar pasta sauce

Shredded Cheese

Fresh Basil

*Directions:*

Line shallow baking dish with some of the pasta sauce, being sure to coat the bottom.

Add zucchini medallions, then add more sauce.

Add some fresh basil and then sprinkle cheese.

Continue this process; then bake at 350 for 10 minutes or until cheese is fully melted.

Serve with garlic bread and enjoy!

# SEMI-HOMEMADE PASTA SAUCE

*This is a quick sauce that you can use in a pinch if you do not have any pasta sauce on hand.*

*Ingredients:*

1 can Tomato Paste

1 White Onion chopped fine

1 Bell Pepper (green, yellow, orange or red) chopped fine

2 cloves of Garlic minced

1-2 TBSP Maple Syrup or Honey

1 TBSP Balsamic Vinegar

1 to 1 ½ cups Water

2 Tsp Oregano

2 Tsp Basil

Olive Oil

Salt/Pepper to taste

*Directions:*

Sauté onions, pepper, and garlic until onions are translucent and soft in skillet on low flame. Cut tomatoes in half and remove seeds. Dice tomatoes and add to the onion mixture. Add tomato paste. Add in water. Cook on low-medium flame. Add more water depending on how thin or thick you want the sauce to be. Add all the spices and sugar and simmer for approximately 35-40 minutes.

*** This makes approximately 3 cups.

Red Onion, Vine ripened Tomatoes, Garlic, Basil & Thyme

Saaudiah Muhammad

**Semi-Homemade Pasta Sauce garnished with fresh basil**

# Zoodles and "Meatballs"

*Ingredients:*

2-3 Zucchinis

Lentil Meatballs (see recipe)

Semi-Homemade Pasta Sauce

Olive Oil to drizzle

*Directions:*

Use spiralizer to create zucchini "noodles". Transfer zoodles into a skillet. Add pasta sauce, making sure to cover fully the zoodles in cause. Warm on low heat. Add lentil meatballs. Continue warming for until zucchini, sauce and meatballs are fully warmed. Enjoy!

**Finished Zoodles and "Meatballs" (top photo), Lentil Meat-balls (bottom left photo), Zoodles**

**Finished Zoodles and Meatballs**

# ZUCCHINI BURGERS

*Ingredients:*

3 cups grated Zucchini (approximately 2 Zucchinis)

1 minced Garlic

1 small Bell Pepper

1 large Egg

1 ½ cups of all-purpose Flour

¼ cup Milk or Half and Half

1 heaping Tablespoon Mayonnaise

2 TSP Onion Powder

1 TSP each dried Basil, Paprika, Salt

Cayenne Pepper to taste

*Directions:*

Combine in a bowl grated zucchini. Mince garlic clove. Finely chop 1 small bell pepper. Add dried basil, salt, pepper, paprika, and onion powder, and mix well. Add milk, then egg. Add 1 ½ cup of all-purpose flour. The mixture will be slightly wet.

Drop spoonfuls into a frying pan with olive oil on medium heat. Flatten the zucchini mixture so it looks like a patty. Cook until golden brown on both sides. Serve on a bun with all of the burger fixings.

**Zucchini Burger on whole wheat bun topped with cheese & dill pickle.**

# THE WONDERFUL WORLD OF MIXED VEGETABLES!

**This section will highlight dishes with single or multiple vegetables as the star of the show.**

**There are some staple vegetables that I almost always cook with such as bell peppers, onions, and garlic. These staple vegetables are definitely the start of a great meal!**

**Did you know?** *Red bell peppers also contain lycopene, which is a carotene that*
*helps to protect against cancer and heart disease. Possibly due to their vitamin C and beta carotene content, bell peppers have been shown to be protective against cataracts. Just like other nutrient-dense vegetables, bell peppers contain many different powerful phytochemicals. Bell peppers have also been shown to prevent blood clot formation and reduce the risk of heart attacks and*
*strokes probably due to their content of substances such as vitamin C, capsaicin, and*

*flavonoids.*

**Did you know?** *Cauliflower is an excellent source of fiber, which helps to improve colon health and can even help prevent cancer. Studies have shown* **carrots** *reduce the risk of lung cancer, breast cancer, and colon cancer. Researchers have just discovered falcarinol and falcarindiol which they feel cause the anticancer properties.* **Eggplants** *are rich in fiber and are low in soluble carbohydrates, those with type 2 diabetes could also benefit from it by adopting an eggplant-based diet. It controls the glucose absorption of the body and it also helps reduce hypertension.*

# STUFFED PEPPERS

*Ingredients:*

4 Bell Peppers (Use a variety of colors of colors if possible)

2 cups of cooked Rice or Quinoa

1 can of diced Tomatoes (14.5 oz)

1/2 to 1 cup Cheese (Cheddar, Colby, Swiss etc.)

1 large Broccoli florets steamed and cut in small pieces

1 Garlic clove minced

1 medium White Onion

1 TBSP Oregano

1/2 TSP Cumin

1 TBSP dried Basil

2 TSP dried Thyme

2 TBSP Butter

Salt and Pepper to taste

*Directions:*

Preheat oven to 400.

Cut the tops of the peppers and scoop out the seeds. Set aside. Sauté onion until translucent in butter. Combine cooked rice with finely chopped broccoli, onions, garlic, cheese, and spices. Add diced tomatoes. Place the rice mixture in the peppers. Make sure the peppers are standing upright in a lightly greased baking dish. Bake for about 25-30 minutes. Enjoy!

# SAAUDIAH'S EASY AND QUICK ALOO GOBI (SISTER GIRL STYLE :-)

*Ingredients:*
1 head of Cauliflower
Red Potatoes (5 or 6 average sized or maybe 10 small) diced
2 TBSP Olive Oil/Butter
2 TSP Fresh Ginger Root grated/dried ginger if fresh isn't available
1 TBSP Curry Powder
¼ cup Milk/ Cream
Salt taste
Cayenne Pepper to taste

Directions:
Boil Cauliflower until tender/done (about 6-8 minutes). Boil potatoes until done. Combine cauliflower and potatoes. Begin to smash/mash both. Add just a little cream just to smooth out the consistency. There should be plenty of texture. Add spices including the grated ginger. Add olive oil/ butter to brighten the aloo gobi and enjoy!

**Did you know?** *Folate is also found in cauliflower, which is a B vitamin that is needed for cell growth and replication. For this reason, it is often recommended that women who are pregnant or may become pregnant eat significant amounts of cauliflower in order to help their unborn children develop properly.*

# MEDITERRANEAN VEGETABLES WITH CREAMY GARLIC YOGURT SAUCE

*Ingredients:*

1 Small Cauliflower

1 Medium Eggplant

3-4 Carrots

2-3 Cloves of Garlic

1 TBSP Nutmeg

1 TBSP Cinnamon

1 TBSP Black Pepper

2 TSP Salt

1 ½ cup of Greek Yogurt

Olive Oil

*Directions:*

Preheat oven to 400 degrees.

Cut cauliflower in small pieces and place in a bowl. Cut eggplant in 1/2 rounds; add to cauliflower. Peel carrots and cut into no more than a 1/4-inch round; add into the vegetable mix.

Coat the vegetables with olive oil, making sure every area is coated. In a small bowl add nutmeg, cinnamon, pepper, and salt. Set aside 1 1/2 teaspoon. Coat the olive oil vegetables with the spice mixture. Place the coated vegetables in a greased roasting pan, making sure vegetables have room to move. Coat garlic with olive oil and add to the roasting pan.

Roast for 20 minutes or until done.

Note: Garlic may cook sooner, make sure you check on the cloves. The vegetables should be tender and browned. Serve over brown rice or quinoa, with *Creamy Garlic Sauce*.

Feast away!!!!

**Creamy Garlic Yogurt Sauce:** Blend together yogurt, spices, and chopped roasted garlic. Serve over vegetables.

# VEGETABLE FUSILLI PASTA WITH GARLIC CREAM

*Ingredients:*

2 cups Fusilli Pasta (Whole Wheat)

1 large Broccoli Floret cut in small pieces

2 medium Carrots thinly sliced

1 medium to large Red, Yellow or Orange Pepper *(Green if no other colors are available)*

1 medium White Onion

3 Tablespoon Sun-dried Tomatoes

3 large cloves Garlic

4 Tablespoon Butter

Olive Oil

1/2 cups Unbleached Flour

2 to 3 cups Half and Half/Whole Milk

¼ cup Parmesan Cheese

1 TBSP Basil

1 TBSP Thyme

Salt and cracked Black Pepper to taste

*Directions:*

Preheat oven to 400.

Coat garlic with olive oil and roast for 20 min or until fully roasted. Set aside. Follow directions on the pasta package. Drain and set aside. Sauté all vegetables lightly in olive oil with herbs. The broccoli should still be bright green and slightly crispy, onions should be translucent, carrots soft but not mushy and the peppers should be slightly tender. Set vegetables aside.

In a skillet on low heat melt butter or Earth Balance Spread. Stir in flour and immediately add in the almond or hemp milk. Stir slowly but constantly removing the lumps. Add cheese stir until lumps are gone. Chop roasted garlic and add in cream mixture. Add salt to the cream sauce as or if needed. Add in the vegetables and simmer for 5 minutes.

Add the mixture to the pasta. If the mixture is too thick add in some additional milk or cream to thin it out. Toss in the sun-dried tomatoes. Serve and delight in this creamy pasta dish!

# CURRIED STIR FRY

*Ingredients:*

½ Small Green Cabbage chopped

1 large Broccoli Floret cut in small pieces

2 medium Carrots thinly sliced

1 medium to large Red, Yellow or Orange Pepper (Green if no other colors are available)

1 medium White Onion chopped

1 medium Zucchini grated

1 ½ TBSP Curry

¼ cup Coconut Milk

1 heaping Tablespoon Mayonnaise

Olive Oil to sauté

Salt to Taste

*Directions:*

Combine all the dried spices. In a large skillet on a low to medium flame, coat with olive oil. Add half of the spices. Add the vegetables and sauté until tender. Add coconut milk. Simmer for 10 minutes on medium heat. Add in mayonnaise. Stir in the rest of the spices including salt. More curry can be added if you would like a more curried flavor. Can be served alone or over rice. Everything will be "Irie" after tasting this vegetable combination!

**Did you Know?** *Cabbage also offers a major payoff—the fewest <u>calories</u> and least <u>fat</u> of any <u>vegetable!</u>*

# ROASTED ASPARAGUS WITH HONEY MUSTARD SAUCE

*Ingredients:*
1 bunch of Asparagus
Olive Oil
**Honey Mustard Sauce/Salad Dressing**

*Directions for asparagus:*
Preheat oven to 400.
Place washed and trimmed asparagus in a baking dish and roast for 10 minutes.

**Honey Mustard Sauce (Salad Dressing)**
*Ingredients:*
1 heaping TBSP Dijon Mustard
1 heaping TBSP Mayonnaise/plain yogurt
2 TBSP Cream/Raw Milk
Raw Honey to taste

*Directions:*
Combine all ingredients in a blender. Adjust the ingredients to thicken, thin or make sweeter.

Serve over asparagus or as a salad dressing.

# RED POTATO "PANCAKES"

*Ingredients:*

2 cups Mashed Potatoes

1 Egg

2 Green Onions chopped finely

1 clove of Garlic grated

1-2 TBSP of Milk/Cream

Olive Oil

*Directions:*

Combine all ingredients together, then drop into hot oil for frying.

You can serve with sour cream or alone.

# EGGPLANT BURGERS

*Ingredients:*
1 large Eggplant grated
1 Garlic clove, minced
1 beaten Egg
1 small Red Pepper
1 small White Onion
1 cup (slightly less) of all-purpose Flour
¼ cup Water
1 TSP Oregano
1 TSP Paprika
1 TSP Onion Powder
Dried Basil to taste
Salt to taste
Red pepper to taste
Olive Oil

*Directions:*
Sauté onion and red peppers together, cool. Add mixture to grated eggplant. Add spices. Combine in milk. Add beaten egg.
Stir in flour ¼ cup at a time. Add in flour until the mixture can be formed into patties.
Fry patties until done on each side 3 to 5 minute each side.
Serve on the side with vegetables or on a bun with burger fixings. Bon Appetit!!

# WILD RICE WITH DRIED CRANBERRIES

*This recipe was inspired from a brunch I attended and I LOVE this rice.*

*Ingredients:*

2 cups of Wild Rice

1 cup of organic dried Cranberries

½ Vegetable Bouillon Cube

Salt to taste

*Directions:*

This recipe is as simple as it sounds. Cook rice according to directions and add the bouillon cube. Toss in cranberries and mix well. Serve.

This rice can be served warm or delicious at room temperature.

# "Candied" Corn"

*This pairs nicely with any savory dishes.*

*Ingredients:*

3 ears of fresh Corn on the cob

1 Red Pepper chopped fine

Saaudiah Muhammad

1-2 TBSP Raw Honey
Paprika to taste
Salt to taste
Olive oil for frying

*Directions:*
Cut corn straight from the cob and place in frying pan with olive oil.
Add red pepper and paprika.
Stir in honey and enjoy!

# "Breaded" Okra

*Ingredients:*
1 Bunch of Okra
¾ cup Unbleached Flour
¾ cup Farina
1 TSP Paprika
1 TSP Salt
White Pepper to taste
1 Egg

⅓ cup Water
Olive Oil to drizzle

*Directions:*

Preheat oven to 350. Wash, clean and cut the ends of the okra. Cut okra in half, set aside.

Mix the flours together with the spices. Beat the egg and add the water.

Dip okra in the egg wash then dip in the seasoned flour, then place in well-greased shallow pan.

Once all the okra has been coated with flour in the pan, drizzle olive oil on the pan.

Cook for 35 minutes or until done (the outside is crispy and golden brown.)

# SAAUDIAH'S BEST GUACAMOLE EVER!

*Ingredients:*
2 large Avocado
2 Roma tomatoes seeded and diced
3 green onions chopped
½ Lime (small)
Sea Salt to taste

*Directions:*
Mash avocado. Combine mashed avocado, onions, and tomatoes.
Squeeze lime juice into mixture and add salt to taste.
Serve with tortilla chips and *Ole'*!

**Did you Know?** *The high levels of folate in **avocado** are also protective against strokes. People who eat diets rich in folate have a much lower risk of stroke than those who don't.*

# SALAAM POTATOES

*These potatoes bring back of fond memories of the Salaam Restaurant and the wonderful Sunday buffet. This is my replication of these delectable and memorable potatoes. Enjoy!*

*Ingredients:*

1 ½-2 lb Red Potatoes cut in small cubes

3-4 Cloves of Garlic minced

1 TBSP Paprika

1 TSP Garlic Powder

1 Sprig of Fresh Rosemary (or 2 TSP dried)

4-5 Sprigs of Fresh Thyme (1 ½ TSP)

Salt to Taste

Cayenne Pepper to taste

Olive Oil

*Directions:*

Preheat oven to 425. Grease baking dish and set aside. Coat cubed potatoes in the olive oil well. Add in minced garlic and all the herbs and spices. Place in baking dish and bake for 45 minutes or until done. The skin should be crispy on the outside and tender on the inside.

Note: Try to use fresh Rosemary and Thyme. Using fresh herbs enhances the flavor of this dish.

Saaudiah Muhammad

**Salaam Potatoes pictured with fresh thyme and rosemary.**

# VEGETARIAN DRESSING/ STUFFING

*Ingredients:*

**Farina Bread**

1 Cup All-Purpose Flour

¾ Cup Farina

¾ Cups Milk or Water

¾ TSP Salt

2 ½ TSP Baking Powder

1/3 Cup Olive Oil or Melted Butter

1 Egg

3 TBSP Brown Sugar/ Maple Syrup/Honey

------------------------------------------------------------------------

1 Green Bell Pepper

1 White Onion

4 Stalks Celery chopped fine

1 to 2 TBSP Poultry Seasoning

4 TBSP Butter

2 Cup Vegetable Stock

3 TBSP Flour

1 1/2 to 2 cups Water

Salt/Pepper to taste

3 Field Roast Smoked Apple Sage Sausage (optional)

*Directions:*

Preheat oven to 400.

Combine all ingredients for the farina bread.  Bake in a greased pan 20 minutes.  Set aside and cool.  Sauté onion, bell pepper and celery in butter. Add in apple sage sausages. Add in 3 TBSP flour and quickly add in water. Stir until mixture is thoroughly mixed with no lumps. Simmer for 5 minutes. Set aside.

In a large bowl, crumble the cooled farina bread. Add the apple sausage mixture. Add in the vegetable stock. Add in the poultry seasoning (add 2 TBSP if you would like it more savory) and salt and pepper to taste.

The mixture should be thick but not too thick. Pour mixture into a buttered baking dish and cook for 15 minutes. Serve with cranberry sauce.

# NAVY BEAN TACO DIP

*Ingredients:*

2 cups Navy Beans cooked and drained

2 TBSP Taco Seasonings

1 can Organic Fire Roasted Tomatoes

2 Avocados diced

1 can Black Olives (drained and chopped)

2 -3 cups shredded Cheddar Cheese

Sour Cream

2 TBSP Olive Oil

Shredded Lettuce

Puree navy beans with taco seasonings and olive oil. Layer bean mixture in a baking dish. Add diced avocados on top of beans. Layer lettuce on top of avocados. Add olives. Next, layer with fire roasted tomatoes. Cover with sour cream. Top with cheese.

This is a fun dish for your next get-together. Serve with tortilla chips.

# SHAVED BRUSSEL SPROUTS

*Ingredients:*
1 lb Shaved Brussel Sprouts
3 cloves Garlic
2 TBSP Butter
1 heaping TBSP Mayonnaise
1 TBSP Dijon Mustard
Cracked Black Pepper
Salt to taste

*Directions:*

Melt butter in a skillet over a low flame. Mince garlic and add to the melted butter. Be careful not to burn the garlic. Add Brussel sprouts to butter and cook for approximately 5-7 minutes on medium flame. When the Brussel sprouts are done, add the mayonnaise and mustard, mixing thoroughly. Serve these Brussel sprouts while still warm and top with the black pepper.

*Note: This recipe was inspired by a vegetarian restaurant I visited a few years ago in Detroit. Brussel Sprouts have gotten a bad rap as a vegetable and I wanted to do them justice with this simple and delicious side.*

Tip: I use Brussel sprouts that's already shaved. You can make your own by using your food processor, however. The packaged shaved Brussel sprouts save a bit on the cleanup and time.

**Shaved Brussel Sprouts with cracked black pepper**

# THE WONDERFUL WORLD OF SOUPS!

**Soups are a great and hearty way to have a nice full meal without all the fuss. It can also be the start of a first-class gourmet meal. Soups are made by usually boiling or simmering vegetables, fish or meat with other ingredients. Of course, all these soups are vegetarian and delicious!!!!**

**Did you know?** *Quinoa* is called a "super grain." Some of the nutrients in quinoa include:

- Complete protein. Quinoa contains all 9 essential amino acids that are required by the body as building blocks for muscles.
- Magnesium helps relax your muscles and blood vessels and effects blood pressure. Quinoa contains high levels of this vital nutrient.
- Fiber. Quinoa is a wonderful way to ensure that you consume valuable fiber that eases elimination and tones your colon.
- Manganese and copper. Quinoa is a good source of these minerals that act as antioxidants in your body to get rid of dangerous cancer and disease-causing substances.

Compared to other grains, quinoa is higher in calcium, phosphorus, magnesium, potassium, iron, copper, manganese, and zinc than wheat, barley, or corn.

Studies have shown that quinoa has documented health benefits too! Quinoa, in its whole grain form, may be effective in preventing and treating these conditions:

- Atherosclerosis
- Breast cancer
- Diabetes

- Insulin resistance

Researchers attribute the health benefits of quinoa to its complete nutritional makeup. Quinoa is close to one of the most complete foods in nature because it contains amino acids, enzymes, vitamins and minerals, fiber, antioxidants, and phytonutrients.

# RED LENTIL SOUP

*This soup has more of a stew consistency. You may add more water or vegetable stock for a thinner soup consistency.*

*Ingredients:*

2 cups of Red Lentils

1 Red pepper diced small

1 Red Onion (large) diced small

3 cloves of Garlic

1/3 cup Olive Oil

½ can of Tomato Paste

2 quarts of Water

Red Pepper to taste

2 TSP Cumin

2 TSP Paprika

Fresh Thyme and Basil if available

Vegetable Bouillon (optional)

Salt to taste

*Directions:*

Sauté onions, peppers, and garlic in olive oil in a large stockpot. Add spices; add rinsed lentils to the sautéed vegetables. Add the 8 cups of water. Cook on low flame.

The soup will cook in 25- 35 minutes, cooking on a medium-high flame. Add fresh basil and thyme in the last few minutes of cooking for the freshest flavor. Garnish with cheese.

For a heartier soup try adding *quinoa* in with the rinsed red lentils to thicken the soup and add a new taste dimension.

# CREAMED CAULIFLOWER SOUP

*This soup is super rich and creamy! It is great for a chilly fall or winter evening.*

*Ingredients:*

1 head large of Cauliflower

1 cup of Vegetable Stock

½ TSP Nutmeg

2 Green Onion chopped (for garnish)

3 to 4 cups of cream

4 TBSP Butter

Salt and Pepper to taste

*Directions:*

Cut the cauliflower in smaller florets and cook until tender.

Add the cooked pieces to the blender with the stock and 2 cups of cream. Blend until you reach the desired thickness. Then, add the next cup of cream—at this point, the soup may be at your desired thickness, if so, add in the spices and serve.

Garnish with green onion pieces.

**Did you know?** *Cauliflower is a member of the 'white' family in terms of fruits and vegetables. Included in this group are other natural foods such as bananas, mushrooms, onions, and garlic. Cauliflower contains allicin, which can improve heart health and reduce the risk of strokes, and selenium, a chemical that works well with Vitamin C to strengthen the immune system. Cauliflower can also help to maintain a healthy cholesterol level.*

# CREAM OF ASPARAGUS SOUP

*Ingredients:*
1 bunch of Asparagus
1 cup Vegetable Stock
3 Green Onions chopped finely
2-3 cups of Half and Half
2 TBSP Butter for sautéing
Salt and Pepper to taste

*Directions:*
Wash and chop asparagus into small pieces. In a stock pot, sauté green onions in butter; add a pinch of salt and pepper. Add asparagus. Add vegetable stock; keep the heat on low. Add vegetable bouillon cube (if it has salt, then omit salt in the beginning). Simmer until asparagus is tender—add cream at this point.

Combine all contents in blender and puree until smooth. Add additional cream or water to "thin" out the soup.

Serve with a garnish of cheese or asparagus pieces.

**Did you know?** *Asparagus is high in folate which is now known to be an important protection against cancer. **Note:** Folate is found naturally in leafy green vegetables and citrus fruits. While folic acid is said to be the same as folate, folic acid is the supplemental form. It is always recommended that you get health benefits from eating healthy whole foods.*

# SAAUDIAH'S BLACK BEAN CHILI

*This is a yummy soup to have on a cold wintery day.*

*Ingredients:*

2 cups of Black Bean

1 large Onion chopped fine

3 medium Carrots chopped

3 Celery Stalks

3 cloves Garlic

1 can Tomato Paste

1-16 oz can Fire Roasted Tomatoes

1 TBSP *each* of Cumin, Paprika

2 TBSP Chili Powder

1- 2 Tbsp Maple Syrup or Honey

⅓ cup Olive Oil

1 cup Corn (frozen or canned)

Salt and Cayenne Pepper to taste

2 quarts of water

*Directions:*

Make sure bean have been cleaned and soaked overnight. Add oil in large stock pot over low heat. Chop carrots, celery, and onions in small pieces. Add carrots to the pot to allow them to sauté. Add remaining chopped vegetable. Add spices. Drain beans and rinse in warm water to remove all dirt and debris. Combine rinsed beans to the stock pot with 2 quarts of water. Add maple syrup, corn, fire roasted tomatoes and tomato paste. Turn heat to medium-high. Place lid, slightly ajar on pot. Allow soup to cook for 2 ½ -3 hours, till beans are soft. Add salt and pepper once the soup is done to taste. Add condiments such as cheese or sour cream.

This soup can be prepared traditionally. Sauté all vegetables in olive oil. Add spices. Add beans, water, and tomatoes and paste in the stockpot. Cook on medium heat for 2 ½ -3 hours until soup has thickened and the beans are fully cooked.

Serve with **Farina Bread** (see the recipe for Vegetable Dressing) or **Cheese Herb Bread**. Top with avocado, sour cream and cheese if you'd like.

Tip: Make sure the Black Beans are FRESH. Stale beans will take longer than the recommended cooking time and will not fully cook.

**Black Bean Chili topped with sour cream, avocado, and cheddar cheese.**

# CHEESE HERB BREAD

*Ingredients:*

¾ cup Wheat Flour

1 cup Unbleached Flour

1 large Egg

2 ½ TSP Baking Powder

1/4 cup Olive Oil or Butter

1 ½ cup Milk *or Water*

2 Tbsp Honey/Maple Syrup

1 tsp Salt

1 ½ tsp. each of dried Basil, Oregano, and Thyme

1 ½ to 2 cup Cheese **(use your choice of cheese)**

*Directions:*

Preheat oven to 350 degrees.

Combine all dry ingredients; add wet items.  Pour mixture into greased baking pan (8 x 8).   Bake for approximately 30 minutes. Serve with a side of soup or eat by itself with some butter.

Most of the recipes in the cookbook can be altered to be vegan or gluten-free. Here are some websites for products you may use to substitute the original ingredients. Here are some of my favorite websites:

www.daiyafoods.com

www.udisglutenfree.com

www.cooks.com

www.allfood.com

www.gfree.com

www.allrecipes.com

Saaudiah Muhammad

## About the Author:

Saaudiah Muhammad is a therapist who has her Masters of Science in Social Administration (Social Work). She has enjoyed cooking and baking for many years. Though she is not a professional chef, cooking is more than a hobby, and it brings her joy and she loves seeing others take delight in her food. She has enjoyed a meat-free diet and creating delectable dishes as a result of her love for cooking. Cooking is a form of self-care for Muhammad. She strives to live a natural and holistic lifestyle. In addition to cooking and baking, she is a trained doula and a Reiki practitioner. She enjoys traveling, art, collecting crystals, estate sale shopping and thrifting. She recently started a blog, "The Muslim Therapist" that looks to help reduce the stigma attached to mental health and therapy.

Made in the USA
Las Vegas, NV
10 November 2022

59072708R00038